That's My Dog!

I HAVE A BULLDOG

By Benjamin Proudfit

Gareth Stevens
PUBLISHING

Please visit our website, www.garethstevens.com. For a free color catalog of all our high-quality books, call toll free 1-800-542-2595 or fax 1-877-542-2596.

Library of Congress Cataloging-in-Publication Data
Names: Proudfit, Benjamin author
Title: I have a bulldog / Benjamin Proudfit.
Description: Buffalo, New York : Gareth Stevens Publishing, [2026] | Series: That's my dog! | Includes index | Audience term: Juvenile
Identifiers: LCCN 2024034410 | ISBN 9781482469943 ebook | ISBN 9781482469929 paperback | ISBN 9781482469936 library binding
Subjects: LCSH: Bulldog–Juvenile literature. | Pets–Juvenile literature.
Classification: LCC SF429.B85 P76 2026 | DDC 636.72–dc23
LC record available at https://lccn.loc.gov/2024034410

First Edition

Published in 2026 by
Gareth Stevens Publishing
2544 Clinton Street
Buffalo, NY 14224

Editor: Kristen Nelson
Designer: Leslie Taylor

Photo credits: Cover, pp. 1, 9, 24 (fur) Irene Miller/Shutterstock.com; pp. 5, 13 (face), 24 (wrinkles) Ammit Jack/Shutterstock.com; p. 7 (top left) Josh Namdar/Shutterstock.com, (top right) rebeccaashworthearle/Shutterstock.com, (bottom left) Wirestock Creators/Shutterstock.com, (bottom right) Olga Aniven/Shutterstock.com; p. 11 Eric Isselee/Shutterstock.com; pp. 13 (bubbles), 24 (wrinkles) ChasIKS/Shutterstock; p. 15 Mykola Romanovskyy/Shuttertstock.com; p. 17 Kev Gregory/Shutterstock.com; p. 19 ArtBBNV/Shutterstock.com; p. 21 Cristina Conti/Shutterstock.com; p. 23 WilleeCole Photography/Shutterstock.com.

Printed in China

CPSIA compliance information: Batch #QS26GS: For further information contact Gareth Stevens, New York, New York at 1-800-542-2595.

Contents

This is my bulldog.
Her name is Daisy.

Bulldogs can be many colors. They can be white, tan, and more.

They have short fur.
The fur is smooth.

Bulldogs have big heads.
They have small ears.

Daisy has wrinkles.
I clean them.
This helps keep my
dog healthy.

Daisy and I take a
walk every day.
We do not go far.
Daisy gets tired!

She likes chew toys.
She likes to tug!

The Guardog
The paper you
get your

Daisy goes inside when it is hot. Bulldogs have to stay cool!

Daisy is sweet.
She loves to be
with people.

My dog is the best.

I love my bulldog!

Words to Know

fur

wrinkles

Index